W9-AOL-814

WITHDRAWN

MONSTERS

Werewolves

by Aaron Sautter

Reading Consultant:
Barbara J. Fox
Reading Specialist
North Carolina State University

Content Consultant:
David D. Gilmore
Professor of Anthropology
Stony Brook University
Stony Brook, New York

Capstone
press

Mankato, Minnesota

Blazers is published by Capstone Press,
151 Good Counsel Drive, P.O. Box 669, Mankato, Minnesota 56002.
www.capstonepress.com

Library of Congress Cataloging-in-Publication Data
Sautter, Aaron.
    Werewolves / by Aaron Sautter.
    p. cm.—(Blazers. Monsters)
    Summary: "A brief explanation of the legendary monsters called
werewolves, including their development through history and their use
in popular culture,"—Provided by publisher.
    Includes bibliographical references and index.
    ISBN-13: 978-0-7368-6444-2 (hardcover)
    ISBN-10: 0-7368-6444-X (hardcover)
    1. Werewolves—Juvenile literature. I. Title. II. Series.
GR830.W4S44 2007
398'.45—dc22   2005037724

Editorial Credits
Jennifer Besel, editor; Juliette Peters, designer; Kelly Garvin, photo
    researcher/photo editor; Bob Lentz, illustrator

Photo Credits
AP/Wide World Photos/Daniel Hulshizer, 28–29
Capstone Press/Gary Sundermeyer, 23; Karon Dubke, cover, 5, 6, 7, 8–9
Fortean Picture Library, 12–13, 15, 18
Getty Images Inc./John Kobal Foundation/Hulton Archive, 25; Steve McAlister, 17
Mary Evans Picture Library, 11
Shutterstock/Brian Upton, 9; Robert C. Tussey III, 22
SuperStock/age fotostock, 16
Supplied by Globe Photos Inc., 26

**Capstone Press would like to thank Tom Brooks and the staff of Meadowbrook
Stables in Mankato, Minnesota, for their help in making this book.**

1 2 3 4 5 6 11 10 09 08 07 06

Table of Contents

A Hunter Stalks Its Prey 4

Legends of the Werewolf 10

Finding Werewolves Today 24

Glossary 30

Read More 31

Internet Sites 31

Index 32

MONSTERS

A Hunter Stalks Its Prey

A hiker walks through the
forest on a chilly, moonlit night.
He doesn't know it, but he is not alone.
Someone or something is following him.

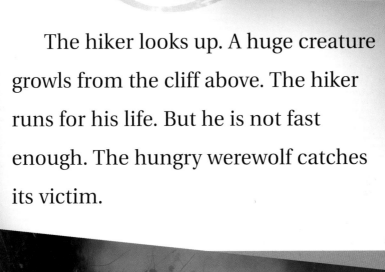

The hiker looks up. A huge creature growls from the cliff above. The hiker runs for his life. But he is not fast enough. The hungry werewolf catches its victim.

The werewolf howls at the moon. In the morning, the monster will return to human form. But at the next full moon it will hunt again.

Legends of the Werewolf

Stories throughout history tell of creatures that are part animal and part human. Ancient Greeks and Romans believed their gods punished people by turning them into animals.

In the 1700s, some people believed magic could turn a person into a werewolf. People who were accused of being werewolves were hunted and killed.

BLAZER FACT

People also believed a person could become a werewolf by drinking water out of a wolf's footprint or by being bitten by a werewolf.

Some diseases can make people look like wolves. But hundreds of years ago, no one knew about these diseases. They believed people who had these diseases were real werewolves.

The members of this family all have a disease that makes them grow long hair all over their bodies.

Stories say people change into werewolves when the moon is full. Long hair sprouts all over their bodies. Their fingernails grow into claws. Their teeth become long, sharp fangs.

17

These imaginary monsters are very dangerous. Werewolves will attack anyone. Stories say most people do not survive a werewolf attack. But if they do, they will turn into a werewolf at the next full moon.

Legend has it that werewolves return to their human form when the sun comes up. They wake up in the woods. They don't know where they are or what they did the night before.

BLAZER FACT

It is said that if a werewolf is wounded, the injury remains after the werewolf changes back to its human form.

Stories explain that only a silver bullet can kill a werewolf. When a werewolf is killed, it returns to its human form. But the person it once was is dead too.

Finding Werewolves Today

Today, we know that werewolves are not real. But werewolf stories still entertain us. Many movies have been made about werewolves.

BLAZER FACT

The *Wolf Man* was a popular werewolf movie in 1941. Many modern werewolf legends are traced to this film.

Werewolves in modern movies take many forms. Some werewolves walk on two legs and dress like people. Others run across the screen on all four legs like real wolves.

Werewolves have scared people for thousands of years. But they are just made-up monsters. It is still fun to use werewolf stories to entertain your friends.

Glossary

accuse (uh-KYOOZ)—to say someone has done something wrong

ancient (AYN-shunt)—very old

imaginary (i-MAJ-uh-ner-ee)—existing in the mind and not in the real world

legend (LEJ-uhnd)—a story handed down from earlier times

sprout (SPROUT)—to grow or develop suddenly or quickly

victim (VIK-tuhm)—a person who is hurt, killed, or made to suffer

MONSTERS

Read More

Allman, Toney. *Werewolves.* Monsters. San Diego: KidHaven Press, 2004.

Hirschmann, Kris. *Werewolves.* Mysterious Encounters. San Diego: KidHaven Press, 2006.

Oxlade, Chris. *The Mystery of Vampires and Werewolves.* Can Science Solve? Chicago: Heinemann, 2002.

Internet Sites

FactHound offers a safe, fun way to find Internet sites related to this book. All of the sites on FactHound have been researched by our staff.

Here's how:

1. Visit *www.facthound.com*

2. Choose your grade level.

3. Type in this book ID **073686444X** for age-appropriate sites. You may also browse subjects by clicking on letters, or by clicking on pictures and words.

4. Click on the **Fetch It** button.

FactHound will fetch the best sites for you!

Index

diseases, 14, 15

features of werewolves, 16, 27
forests, 4, 21
full moon, 9, 16, 19

human form, 9, 21, 22

killing werewolves, 12, 22

legends, 10, 16, 19, 21, 22, 24, 28

magic, 12
movies, 24, 27

silver bullets, 22
stories (see legends)
sun, 21

turning into werewolves, 12, 16, 19

victims, 7

werewolf attacks, 19
woods (see forests)